Protect
Nature

Kay Barnham

Crabtree Publishing Company
www.crabtreebooks.com

Crabtree Publishing Company

www.crabtreebooks.com

Editors: Penny Worms, Molly Aloian, Michael Hodge
Senior Design Manager: Rosamund Saunders
Designer: Ben Ruocco, Tall Tree Ltd

Photo Credits:
Alamy images: p. 18 (John White Photos). Corbis images: p. 19 (Galen Rowell), p. 21 (Grace/zefa). Ecoscene: title page and p. 12 (Reinhard Dirscherl), p. 5 (Frank Blackburn), p. 6 (David Wootton Photography), p. 7 (Kjell Sandved), p. 9 (Reinhard Dirscherl), p. 10 (Luc Hosten), p. 13 (Andy Binns), p. 14 (Wayne Lawler), p. 15 (Robert Baldwin), p. 17 (Edward Bent), p. 22 (Stephen Coyne), p. 23 (Satyendra Tiwari), p. 24 (Sally Morgan), p. 25 (Frank Blackburn), p. 26 (Angela Hampton), p. 29 (Angela Hampton). Getty images: p. 4 (Johnny Johnson), p. 8 (Michael S Quinton), p. 11 (Michael Kelley), p. 16 (Daryl Balfour), p. 27 (Arthur Tilley). Photolibrary: cover and p. 28 (Satushek Steve). Wayland Picture Library: p. 20.

Library and Archives Canada Cataloguing in Publication

Barnham, Kay
    Protect nature / Kay Barnham.

(Environment action)
Includes index.
ISBN 978-0-7787-3658-5 (bound).--ISBN 978-0-7787-3668-4 (pbk.)

    1. Nature conservation--Juvenile literature. 2. Environmental protection--Juvenile literature. I. Title. II. Series: Barnham, Kay. Environment action.

QH75.B36 2007   j333.95'16   C2007-904690-8

Library of Congress Cataloging-in-Publication Data

Barnham, Kay.
    Protect nature / Kay Barnham.
        p. cm. -- (Environment action)
    Includes index.
    ISBN-13: 978-0-7787-3658-5 (rlb)
    ISBN-10: 0-7787-3658-X (rlb)
    ISBN-13: 978-0-7787-3668-4 (pbk)
    ISBN-10: 0-7787-3668-7 (pbk)
    1. Nature conservation--Juvenile literature. I. Title. II. Series.

QH75.B287 2008
333.95'16--dc22
                                        2007029998

Crabtree Publishing Company

www.crabtreebooks.com   1-800-387-7650

Printed in China/042011/CP20110131

Published in Canada
Crabtree Publishing
616 Welland Ave.
St. Catharines, Ontario
L2M 5V6

Published in the United States
Crabtree Publishing
PMB 59051
350 Fifth Ave., 59th Floor
New York, NY 10118

Published by CRABTREE PUBLISHING COMPANY
Copyright © **2008**

Contents

All about nature

Nature is the word used to describe the world around us. Natural things are not made by people. Plants, animals, water, and the **landscape** are all parts of nature.

△ The best place to see nature at its most beautiful is far away from people, such as in the Canadian wilderness.

You can see nature in towns and cities, too. Trees, flowers, and insects are all parts of nature. The next time you are outside, take a look around. How many natural things can you see around you?

△ Even the smallest flowers and insects are parts of nature.

Is nature in danger?

Millions of people live on Earth. They need space to live and food to eat. They use **fuel** to heat their homes and run their cars. They make paper from trees and use land for farming. They throw away garbage. All of these **human activities** put nature in danger.

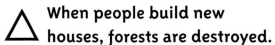 When people build new houses, forests are destroyed.

Giant pandas live in bamboo forests. Huge areas of bamboo forests have been cut down. As a result, giant pandas are in danger of becoming extinct.

Natural habitats are places where animals and plants live. When their natural habitats are changed or destroyed, the animals and plants have to move or adapt. Some may become **extinct**. Animals that are extinct are gone forever.

Climate change

Earth is getting warmer. Many experts believe that this climate change is caused by **carbon dioxide** from power stations, factories, houses, airplanes, and cars. Carbon dioxide is released into Earth's **atmosphere**, trapping the sun's heat. Deserts may get bigger. Sea levels may rise and flood low areas of land.

American pikas are small animals that live on cool mountains. If the temperature of Earth continues to rise, these animals may become extinct.

FACT!

Some scientists believe that **global warming** could threaten over one million animal and plant **species**.

Warm ocean temperatures harm **coral** that lives in tropical oceans and seas. Coral is **fragile**. If the water becomes too warm, the colorful coral fades and dies. Warm water also leads to more powerful **hurricanes** and storms. Hurricanes and storms can cause serious damage to coral.

△ Coral reefs are home to a lot of different animals.

A cleaner world

Pollution can cause great harm to animals and natural habitats. For example, when factories pour **poisonous waste** into oceans, seas, rivers, and lakes, fish and other animals may become sick or die. Many people are working hard to stop water from becoming polluted.

△ Plastic garbage dumped into oceans can kill birds and other animals. The animals may be choked, poisoned or strangled by the garbage.

△ Food wrappers and drink cans cause most of the litter that you see in nature. Take the litter home and recycle it!

Garbage can take hundreds of years to break down and disappear. Some garbage never breaks down. By **reducing**, **reusing**, and **recycling** waste, we can help to make the Earth a cleaner place.

Natural habitats

People have already destroyed natural habitats to make room for houses and farms. Large areas of **rainforests** have been chopped down to make furniture and paper.

△ Orangutans are in danger of becoming extinct because they are losing their natural habitats.

▷ This picture shows a tree nursery in Nepal. People planted thousands of trees to replace those that were cut down.

When people destroy forests, other problems, such as flooding and mudslides, can occur. If hillsides are bare, rain runs down them very quickly. The rushing water will raise water levels in rivers or wash away soil.

FACT!

In the United States and Canada, hundreds of companies and businesses are taking action to protect forests.

Endangered animals

Giant pandas, tigers, whales, dolphins, rhinos, elephants, turtles, and gorillas are just some animals that are in danger of becoming extinct. Some have been killed for their meat, fur, and tusks. Some have been hunted for sport. Others have lost their habitats.

Some people hunt tigers. Fewer than 500 Sumatran tigers now live in the wild.

Today, **endangered** animals are protected. Most endangered animals live in **nature reserves**, which are areas where they are protected. People are taking important steps to help provide better futures for these animals.

△ In Ecuador, people are using a new type of fishing hook to catch fish. As a result, people are catching far fewer endangered sea turtles by accident.

Nature reserves

In nature reserves, animals come first. The reserves are created to protect the homes of **rare** animals and plants. Park rangers take care of the animals and stop people from harming them.

△ Elephants, impalas, and antelopes are safe in this nature reserve in Namibia, Africa.

Nature reserves are open to the public. Everyone can enjoy the **environment** and see plants and animals in their natural habitats. Visitors are welcome, as long as they leave the nature reserves exactly as they found them.

▽ These tourists are visiting a nature reserve on Skomer Island. It is home to many sea birds and seals.

Marine reserves

Some protected areas are not just on land—they include parts of oceans, seas, lakes, and bays. These **marine reserves** are places where animals can live safely in water. Shipping and fishing are controlled. People are not allowed to drill for oil and gas or dump garbage into the water.

Some types of fish, including these bluefin tuna, are now very rare because of overfishing, habitat loss, and pollution.

There are a lot of marine reserves around the world. Nature lovers would like to see many more, however. Marine reserves are ideal places for people to see nature without spoiling it.

△ Monterey Bay in California is a protected area of sea and coastline. It is home to sea birds, fish, mammals, and plants. This sea otter lives there safely.

19

FACT!

Almost 80 percent of all commercial fish populations, including tuna, marlin, and swordfish, are threatened species.

Stop, think, act!

There are a lot of things that we can do to protect nature, both around the world and closer to home. Before you buy things, make sure that natural habitats or wildlife have not been harmed to make them. For example, if you buy recycled paper, you can be sure that new trees have not been chopped down to make it.

◁ Think before you throw things away! Could you recycle them? Cans, cardboard, batteries, and plastic are just some things that can be recycled.

Many household cleaners contain poisonous **chemicals**. These chemicals harm the environment when they get into the water. Encourage your parents to shop for **environmentally friendly** or "green" products. These products contain chemicals that dissolve or disappear harmlessly in water.

On vacation

Around the world, people work hard to make sure that nature is protected. You can help too! When you are on vacation, choose **souvenirs** carefully. Make sure that endangered animals and natural habitats have not been harmed to make the souvenirs. Ivory ornaments are made from elephant tusks. Hardwood furniture may come from rainforests.

◁ People take coral and sponge from coral reefs to make souvenirs. The people often damage the coral reefs.

When tourists visit animals in nature reserves, they are helping protect nature by giving money to the reserves.

People sometimes capture animals. They sell the animals as pets or make the animals work. They may mistreat the animals. It is very difficult for these animals to learn to live in their natural habitats again. Capturing and selling animals is illegal, and many people are working hard to stop these activities.

At home

There are a lot of ways that you can protect nature at home. If you have a garden, you can make **compost** instead of throwing scrap food away. Fill a composter with scrap food. When the food is rotten and broken down, spread it on soil to feed growing plants.

◁ Teabags, fruit peels, eggshells, and vegetable peels can be composted, along with grass cuttings and leaves.

During the cold winter months, hang a bird feeder outside. The food will help birds survive through winter, when food is hard to find. If you have a cat, make sure that it wears a bell. The sound of the bell will warn the birds!

▽ Use different types of seeds to attract different types of birds.

At school

When you are at school, there are many things that you can do to learn about nature and how to protect it. Some schools have vegetable patches where students grow vegetables. Others have birdwatching clubs where students look for birds and learn about them.

◁ Plant a tree and watch it grow! Pay attention to how it changes from season to season and what animals it attracts.

An easy and important way to protect nature is to make sure that all litter is put into garbage cans or recycled. Litter can make places look ugly and messy, but more importantly, it can harm plants and animals.

△ Picking up litter is one of the easiest ways that you can help protect nature.

FACT!

Small animals can get trapped inside bottles or cans. Broken bottles can cut their feet.

More ideas!

If your parents have a garden or a window box, grow some of your own plants! There are a lot of things that you can add to a garden to encourage plants and animals to live and grow there. Ask a gardener which plants will grow well.

△ Flowers will attract bees, butterflies, and insects. Small trees and bushes will provide shelter for small animals like hedgehogs and frogs.

Use a **water butt** or a bucket to collect rainwater. You can use this water to water your garden when the weather is dry.

Do not use sprays to control weeds. Let weeds grow! Some interesting plants may begin to sprout in your garden.

FACT!

Do not use **peat** to grow plants in pots. People take peat from natural habitats. Use peat-free compost or your own homemade compost.

Glossary

atmosphere The air around Earth

carbon dioxide A type of gas in the air

chemicals Powerful liquids or powders that can be used for many things, including cleaning

compost Rotted vegetables and other waste that is added to soil as food for plants

coral A kind of rock made in oceans and seas from the bodies of tiny animals

endangered Describes animals that are in danger of dying out in the wild

environment The world we live in, especially plants, animals, and nature

environmentally friendly Products that do not harm the environment

extinct Describes animals that are no longer living anywhere on Earth or animals that have not been seen in the wild for at least 50 years

fragile Easily broken

fuel Anything that is burned to make heat

global warming The gradual increase of the Earth's temperature

human activities The things people do

hurricanes Storms with very strong winds

landscape A large area of countryside

marine reserves Safe areas where animals can live in water

natural habitats Places where animals or plants usually live

nature reserves Safe areas where animals can live without being harmed by human activity

peat A type of rich, boggy soil

poisonous waste Leftover chemicals that can cause death or harm

pollution Dirty or unhealthy air, land, or water

rainforest A large forest in a hot part of the world

rare Hard to find

recycling Not throwing something away after use but using it again somehow

reducing Making something smaller or less

reusing Using something again

souvenirs Things that you buy to remind you of a vacation or place

species A type of living thing

water butt A large barrel that catches rainwater

Index